Fa

R

NG

S

DOROS

Raintree is an imprint of Capstone Global Library Limited,
a company incorporated in England and Wales having its registered office at
264 Banbury Road, Oxford, OX2 7DY – Registered company number: 6695582

www.raintree.co.uk
myorders@raintree.co.uk

Edited by Aaron Sautter
Designed by Kyle Grenz
Picture research by Eric Gohl
Production by Steve Walker
Printed and bound in China

ISBN 978 1 474 74458 4
22 21 20 19 18 17
10 9 8 7 6 5 4 3 2 1

British Library Cataloguing in Publication Data
A full catalogue record for this book is available from the British Library.

Acknowledgements
We would like to thank the following for permission to reproduce photographs:
Alamy: Reuters, 8; Kyle Ober: 21; Newscom: EPA/Swen Pfoertner, 5, 18, FEATURECHINA/
Xu Kangping, 13, KRT/Phil Velasquez, 23, picture-alliance/dpa/Peter Steffen, 17, Reuters/Ina
Fassbender, 14, Xinhua News Agency/Sergei Bachlakov, 24, 27, ZUMA Press/Paul Rodriguez,
7; Shutterstock: 11, Illustratiostock, cover (back), KeongDaGreat, 29, Martial Red, cover (right),
Sergei Bachlakov, 28, RealVector, cover (left), Rvector, cover (back)

Every effort has been made to contact copyright holders of material reproduced in this book.
Any omissions will be rectified in subsequent printings if notice is given to the publisher.

0517/CA21700461 042017 4655

CONTENTS ▶

BEING SOMEONE ELSE

Have you ever wanted to be a spy? How about a spell-casting wizard? Or perhaps a soldier or ninja from the future? In role-playing games (RPGs), players can be anyone they choose.

FACT

RPGs can be tabletop games, online games or live-action events.

TABLETOP FUN

▶ In tabletop games, players often use character sheets, dice and **miniatures**. The game master (GM) creates a setting and tells a story. The player characters (PCs) then take actions as part of the story. They roll dice to decide the result of their actions.

miniature – small metal or plastic figure that represents a player's character in a role-playing game

Players enjoying a game of *Dungeons & Dragons*

FACT

Dungeons & Dragons is one of the oldest and most popular role-playing games. Gary Gygax and Dave Arneson introduced it in 1974.

Each year, hundreds of gamers play at the Gen Con Indy convention in Indiana, USA.

FACT

Regional Iron GM winners are called Iron Contenders. They compete for the Iron GM World Championship – and cash prizes.

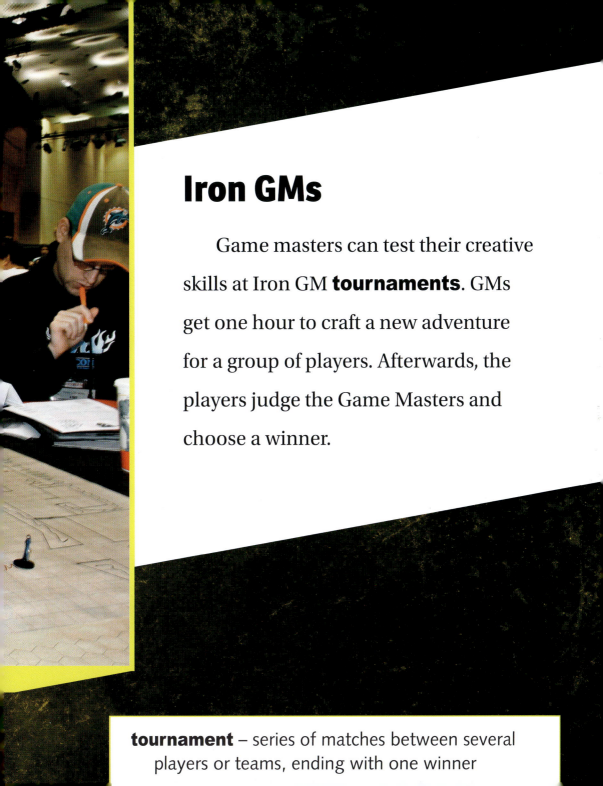

Iron GMs

Game masters can test their creative skills at Iron GM **tournaments**. GMs get one hour to craft a new adventure for a group of players. Afterwards, the players judge the Game Masters and choose a winner.

tournament – series of matches between several players or teams, ending with one winner

RPG Superstar

Every year, Paizo Publishing holds the RPG Superstar contest. Game designers enter information about magic items, spells or maps they've created. The winner earns a chance to work on the company's popular games.

FACT

Paizo Publishing creates popular tabletop RPGs such as *Pathfinder* and *Starfinder*.

A VIRTUAL PLAYGROUND

▶ Massively Multiplayer Online RPGs (MMORPGs) are very popular. Players become **virtual** heroes. They set out to gain experience while completing **quests**. Skilled players can earn big prizes.

virtual – when a location, person or object exists only as part of a computer program

quest – adventure in which a hero tries to achieve a goal

In 2014, the Electronic Sports League (ESL) held a *Prime World* Go4 Cup series. Top scorers won £80 per week. The best players earned £400 in the monthly finals.

WoW

Millions of people around the world play *World of Warcraft* (*WoW*). In the *WoW Arena* World Championship, teams of skilled players battle for the title and the grand prize.

LIVING FANTASY WORLDS

People live inside a story during live action role-playing games, or LARPs. Players can join LARP **guilds** all over the world. These live events usually last from three to five days.

guild – group of people who share similar interests

LARP players wear costumes and use props to bring their characters to life.

FACT

There are two types of LARP players. Player characters (PCs) choose their characters' actions. Non-player characters (NPCs) and storytellers perform pre-written actions that advance the story.

Most LARP players use only safe weapons made of plastic pipe and foam. In battle, they simply try to touch an opponent's arms, legs or chest with their weapons.

Herofest

At Herofest players spend weekends in a magical world. Teams, or **factions**, are made up of warriors, healers and others. Teams complete missions within the story to win.

faction – group of people who work together towards a common goal

Knight Realms

Knight Realms takes place in the imaginary world of Arawyn. Players gather each month in New Jersey, USA, to play in a heroic story. Each year, players win several awards such as Best Combat Roleplayer and Hero of the Year.

dystopian world – imaginary place where people are often poor, hungry and scared

A player dressed as a tree monster at Knight Realms

WANT TO MAKE A TRADE?

▶ Many people enjoy Trading Card Games (TCGs). Players fill their deck with cards that fit their **strategy**. They use the cards to attack opponents and reduce their **hit points**. The last player left is the winner.

strategy – plan for winning a game or contest

hit point – specific number that represents the amount of life a character has in a role-playing game

Magic players use creature and spell cards for attacking and defense.

Magic: The Gathering

Magic: The Gathering is one of the most popular TCGs in the world. Players play cards to cast spells and **summon** creatures to the battlefield. Players take turns to do battle until only one remains.

summon – to command something or someone to appear at a specific place

Magic Grand Prix

Magic players can test their skills at large Grand Prix events around the world. The Top 8 players from each event are invited to the Pro Tour. There they play to win the £40,000 grand prize.

Thousands of *Magic: The Gathering* players compete in Grand Prix events.

Pokémon began in 1996 as a trading card game. Since then, its popularity has spread to video games, cartoons and comic books.

The *Pokémon* craze

The *Pokémon* European International Championships are held each year in London. The event features both TCG and video game competitions. Players compete for cash prizes of up to £200,000.

FACT

Pokémon Go! was released in July 2016. It was a huge hit. Within a month, more than 20 million people were playing the game every day.

Glossary

dystopian world imaginary place where people are often poor, hungry and scared

faction group of people who work together towards a common goal

guild group of people who share similar interests

hit point specific number that represents the amount of life a character has in a role-playing game

miniature small metal or plastic figure that represents a player's character in a role-playing game

quest adventure in which a hero tries to achieve a goal

strategy plan for winning a game or contest

summon to command something or someone to appear at a specific place

tournament series of matches between several players or teams, ending with one winner

virtual when a location, person or object exists only as part of a computer program

Read more

LARP! Volume 1, Dan Jolley and Shawn DeLoache
(Dark Horse, 2015)

*Minecraft: Beginner's Handbook: And Official Minecraft
Book,* Mojang AB (Egmont Publishing UK, 2015)

*Pokémon Deluxe Essential Handbook: The Need-to-Know
Stats and Facts on Over 700 Pokémon,* Cris Silvestri
(Scholastic, 2015)

Websites

www.live-roleplaying.co.uk
Learn more about dressing up and playing as your
favourite characters at Herofest events.

www.dragonmeet.co.uk
Learn all about the yearly convention in London that
features many tabletop games, card games and more.

Index